D0116850

Caesar Rodney

American Patriot

Colonial Leaders

Lord Baltimore
English Politician and Colonist

Benjamin Banneker
American Mathematician and Astronomer

Sir William Berkeley
Governor of Virginia

William Bradford
Governor of Plymouth Colony

Jonathan Edwards
Colonial Religious Leader

Benjamin Franklin
American Statesman, Scientist, and Writer

Anne Hutchinson
Religious Leader

Cotton Mather
Author, Clergyman, and Scholar

Increase Mather
Clergyman and Scholar

James Oglethorpe
Humanitarian and Soldier

William Penn
Founder of Democracy

Sir Walter Raleigh
English Explorer and Author

Caesar Rodney
American Patriot

John Smith
English Explorer and Colonist

Miles Standish
Plymouth Colony Leader

Peter Stuyvesant
Dutch Military Leader

George Whitefield
Clergyman and Scholar

Roger Williams
Founder of Rhode Island

John Winthrop
Politician and Statesman

John Peter Zenger
Free Press Advocate

Revolutionary War Leaders

John Adams
Second U.S. President

Ethan Allen
Revolutionary Hero

Benedict Arnold
Traitor to the Cause

King George III
English Monarch

Nathanael Greene
Military Leader

Nathan Hale
Revolutionary Hero

Alexander Hamilton
First U.S. Secretary of the Treasury

John Hancock
President of the Continental Congress

Patrick Henry
American Statesman and Speaker

John Jay
First Chief Justice of the Supreme Court

Thomas Jefferson
Author of the Declaration of Independence

John Paul Jones
Father of the U.S. Navy

Lafayette
French Freedom Fighter

James Madison
Father of the Constitution

Francis Marion
The Swamp Fox

James Monroe
American Statesman

Thomas Paine
Political Writer

Paul Revere
American Patriot

Betsy Ross
American Patriot

George Washington
First U.S. President

Famous Figures of the Civil War Era

Jefferson Davis
Confederate President

Frederick Douglass
Abolitionist and Author

Ulysses S. Grant
Military Leader and President

Stonewall Jackson
Confederate General

Robert E. Lee
Confederate General

Abraham Lincoln
Civil War President

William Sherman
Union General

Harriet Beecher Stowe
Author of Uncle Tom's Cabin

Sojourner Truth
Abolitionist, Suffragist, and Preacher

Harriet Tubman
Leader of the Underground Railroad

Caesar Rodney

American Patriot

Susan McCarthy Melchiore

Arthur M. Schlesinger, jr.
Senior Consulting Editor

Chelsea House Publishers

Philadelphia

Produced by Pre-Press Company, Inc., East Bridgewater, MA 02333

CHELSEA HOUSE PUBLISHERS
Editor in Chief Stephen Reginald
Production Manager Pamela Loos
Art Director Sara Davis
Director of Photography Judy L. Hasday
Managing Editor James D. Gallagher
Senior Production Editor J. Christopher Higgins

Staff for *CAESAR RODNEY*
Project Editor Anne Hill
Associate Art Director Takeshi Takahashi
Series Design Keith Trego

The Chelsea House World Wide Web address is http://www.chelseahouse.com

First Printing
1 3 5 7 9 8 6 4 2

Library of Congress Cataloging-in-Publication Data

Melchiore, Susan McCarthy
    Caesar Rodney/Susan McCarthy Melchiore
        p. cm. — (Colonial Leaders)
    Includes bibliographical references and index.
    ISBN 0-7910-5968-5 (HC) 0-7910- 6125-6(PB)
        1. Rodney, Caesar, 1728–1784—Juvenile literature. 2. Statesman—United
    States—Biography—Juvenile literature. 3. United States—History—Revolution,
    1775–1783—Juvenile literature. 4. United States. Declaration of Indepen
    dence—Signers—Biography—Juvenile literature. 5. United States. Continental
    Congress—Biography—Juvenile literature. 6. Legislators—Delaware—Biogra
    phy—Juvenile literature. 7. Delaware—History—Revolution, 1775–1783—Juve
    nile literature. [1. Rodney, Caesar, 1728–1784. 2. Statesman. 3. United
    States—History—Revolution, 1775–1783.] I. Title. II. Series

E207.R6 M45 2000
973.3'092—dc21
[B]
                                                                00-038376

> **Publisher's Note:** In Colonial and Revolutionary War America, there were no standard rules for spelling, punctuation, capitalization, or grammar. Some of the quotations that appear in the Colonial Leaders and Revolutionary War Leaders series come from original documents and letters written during this time in history. Original quotations reflect writing inconsistencies of the period.

Contents

The plantation in Delaware where Caesar Rodney was raised required a lot of hard work, even from the children. As a boy, Caesar spent time performing a variety of chores for his family: feeding chickens, pulling weeds, and collecting wood.

Learning to
Be a Leader

It happened in the middle of the night. On October 7, 1728, a cry woke farmer Rodney. It came from his young wife Elizabeth. Their first baby was coming. The farmer sent for help. But the baby didn't wait. Around midnight, a son was born in his father's own hands. The tired man couldn't then know that the future of Delaware lay in his arms.

This had been a terrible year for the farmers in the **colony** of Delaware. A winter flood, summer pests, and drought had killed many animals and ruined crops. The harvest wasn't good. But the new father couldn't help smiling. He reached for his little diary and recorded this wonderful day. "Hung some tobacco. Came in, got dinner and killed some squirrels. . . . ye child was born and it was a SON." The happy parents named their son Caesar, after his father.

Times were hard. Sickness and disease killed many people. Many babies didn't live very long. But Caesar survived, and soon he had two siblings.

Colonial women had to work very hard. They made most of the things they needed— from soap and candles to clothing for the whole family. Caesar's mother wore an apron to protect her clothes. The apron was also a good babysitter. She could tie the long strings to her toddler like a leash, and she could keep working. That way the baby couldn't wander off, and she knew he was safe.

Little Caesar had long hair. He wore clothing that looked like a long dress. People today would think he looked like a girl. But his fashionable parents knew just how to dress him. All colonial parents dressed their young boys this way. They called these dresses coats. Boys stayed "in coats" until they were six or seven. After that they dressed like their fathers. Their tight pants that ended just below the knee were called breeches.

When Caesar was almost out of coats, a little sister was born. Her name was Sarah, and she didn't live more than a year. Caesar loved baby Sarah and was very sad when she died.

A statue of Caesar Rodney stands today in the Capitol building in Washington, D.C. Another, in Wilmington, Delaware, shows him on his horse, watching over Rodney Square. Caesar has been appearing in a lot of other places as well. In 1999, more than 200 years after his death, the people of Delaware chose him to represent his beloved state again. Caesar's image now gallops across the back of the new Delaware state quarter.

When Caesar was seven, another sister came along. Now there were four children in the kitchen at mealtimes.

Caesar helped his parents. There was always plenty to do on the **plantation.** He looked after his brother and sisters. He also helped feed the animals and fetched heavy buckets of water from the well. A large, open fireplace was used for cooking and heating the house. Caesar gathered and chopped wood for the fire.

Some chores changed with the seasons. In spring Caesar learned about plants such as wheat, tobacco, and corn. He learned to plow, plant, hoe, and harvest. Corn was very important. Almost every meal had something made out of corn.

All the children helped take care of the herb garden. It was kept close to the house. The children sowed seed, weeded the garden, and gathered herbs. Mrs. Rodney used the herbs to make medicine. Herbs also made their food more tasty.

In summer Caesar collected berries for his mother. She turned them into pies, drinks, jams, and jellies. He gathered special plants called scouring rushes that grew in the marshes nearby. His mother used them to clean the pewter dishes.

In colonial kitchens, cooking was performed over an open fire. Meat was cooked on a spit, and it usually became the responsibility of one of the family's children to turn the meat as it cooked.

Caesar helped with the oyster harvest. Oysters as big as a man's hand grew in the Delaware Bay. People loved to eat them. The shells had many uses, too. Colonists crushed the shells and added them to the soil. They helped their crops grow better. Shells were used to pave dirt roads. People even used them in their buildings to make mortar to cement together the bricks.

Harvest time was the busiest period of the year. The colonists needed to work fast harvesting the crops at exactly the right time. Rain at the wrong moment could ruin a whole tobacco crop.

Food needed to last until the next growing season. Caesar's family gathered their crops. They stored some crops for the hard winter, and some crops were sold or traded at the market in Dover. And some were put on ships bound for Philadelphia. After the harvest, the colonists celebrated with fiddling, dancing, eating, and drinking.

Even though they worked hard, the children found time for play. They played hopscotch, which they called "scotch hoppers." They enjoyed a game like badminton called "battledores." Another toy was a large wooden circle called a hoop. Caesar could make it roll along the ground as he ran along beside it and gave it taps with a special stick to keep it going. Sometimes it started to get away from him and he had to run really fast to catch it. Caesar also liked to play marbles.

Winter meant time away from working in the fields. Caesar went sledding and skating. He could also spend a little more time at his books. Caesar's parents were well educated and wanted their children to be educated too.

Mrs. Rodney loved to read. She taught Caesar his letters and numbers in the kitchen. There, she could work and give lessons at the same time.

The Rodney plantation was like many others. It was large and far from the closest school. So traveling teachers sometimes came to the plantation. They stayed for a few weeks at a time. They taught the Rodney children how to read, write, and work with numbers. But there was much more education in store for Caesar.

Andrew Hamilton served as attorney for printer John Peter Zenger in his trial for libel in New York.

Caesar was always learning. At night he sat in a warm little seat by the fireplace. He carved whistles and pop-guns with his jackknife. He listened to the grown-ups talk. And he learned many things. He learned about things that even his teachers and schoolbooks couldn't teach him. When he was seven, he learned about a man in New York City named John Peter Zenger and the famous lawyer from Pennsylvania named Andrew Hamilton.

New York had a powerful governor named William Cosby. The king of England had made this corrupt and greedy man governor. New York was stuck with a governor that didn't want to listen to the people.

John Peter Zenger was a printer in New York. He wanted the people to know the bad things the governor was doing. He printed stories in his newspaper that made the governor very mad. The governor put Zenger in jail for almost a year. Finally a day was picked for a trial, but the governor wouldn't let any of Zenger's lawyer friends defend him. Although John Peter Zenger was in big trouble, he had lots of friends and they found a way to help him.

On the day of the trial there was a surprise. Andrew Hamilton, having traveled two weeks from Philadelphia, walked into the courthouse. Zenger's friends had asked him to come. Hamilton argued that Zenger hadn't committed a crime because all of the things he printed were true.

Hamilton and Zenger won the case. This was one of the first important steps toward freedom of the press in the colonies. It meant that printers didn't have to be afraid of printing the truth.

Hamilton's successful defense of John Peter Zenger (above) was a defining moment in establishing freedom of the press in the colonies.

Caesar learned the value of truth. As he grew, he spent more time with his father, who taught him many things. Mrs. Rodney was busy again with a new baby, another brother. Caesar learned how to handle a gun, sail a small boat, and ride a horse.

Mr. Rodney brought Caesar with him on trips. Caesar loved to visit Dover, in Kent County, Delaware. He loved to watch the craftsmen at work. He stopped at the shops of the blacksmith and the shoemaker, and he liked to watch the turner make fancy carved spindles. But his favorite trips were to Philadelphia. It was the largest and most exciting city in the colonies.

In a time long before cars, trains, and planes, travel was difficult, dangerous, and uncomfortable. People often used horses to get around. Most roads were unpaved and extremely bumpy. Travelers arrived shaken and dust-covered. When it rained, mud splattered, horses slipped, and carriages got stuck. Even in good weather, travel was very slow. But bad weather such as rain, snow, or cold could add days or even weeks to a journey. The trip between Dover and Philadelphia often took Caesar two or three days. Today, the same trip can be made by car or bus in about two hours.

On long trips to Philadelphia, Caesar and his father stopped at places called ordinaries. There they ate and drank. The horses rested, and the Rodneys rested too. They met both friends and strangers and talked about news in the colonies. They complained about some of England's laws, like the one that allowed them to make only enough woolen cloth for their family's use. England didn't want the colonies to compete with its own successful clothing business.

Young Caesar learned much from the talk in the ordinaries. But he learned more from his father. His father taught him to manage the plantation. By the time he was 12, Caesar was beginning to handle the plantation on his own, which was useful training for the leader he was to become. He learned how to buy, sell, and trade. Most importantly, he learned how to get along with people. This ability would serve him well in his future work.

At 13, Caesar could read and write and was skilled in Latin. But his parents wanted him to learn even more. They decided to send him away to school in Philadelphia.

Caesar was excited. Philadelphia was a big, beautiful, and interesting city. He was a little scared, too. Philadelphia was far from home. It could take two or three days by horse or ship, depending on the weather. He would be on his own. He wouldn't get to see his family for a long time. But he would get a better education.

So, when he was 14, Caesar packed his bags. He was off to Philadelphia on a new adventure.

Philadelphia was a cultural center for the colonies and an exciting place for young Caesar to visit. He moved to the city in order to attend the Latin School, but learned as much from the city and its busy people as he did from the books he read at school.

Changes
for Caesar

Philadelphia was known as a center of culture and learning. Some of the most respected families in the colonies lived there, too. Thanks to Benjamin Franklin, Philadelphia already had a public library, a fire department, a good post office, and a new school.

Philadelphia's cobblestone streets were full of hustle and bustle. Horses, carriages, people, and carts came and went. Merchants called out in the streets to attract business. Children watched skilled craftspeople make everything from buttons and boots to barrels and boats by hand. Shops of every kind filled

Caesar's father wrote this advice in a letter dated July 16, 1743: "Dear Child be Diligent at your Books and make what progress you possibly Can in Learning while you have an opertunity. I hope youl be Carefull in Chusing your Company. I would have you use all posable means to git in favour with the Better Sort of people, for there is no greater advantage to youth than good Company. Nor No greater Disadvantage than ill."

the air with interesting sights, sounds, and smells.

Watching everyone hard at work made Caesar wonder what he would be when he grew up. Would he be a turner like his father once was, or a farmer? Maybe he'd be an inventor, like Mr. Franklin.

Penn's Landing on the Delaware River was filled with ships from around the world. Caesar liked to go and see what the ships brought in. It was a special day when his family's **shallop** sailed up the river with news and letters from home.

One letter in July 1743, brought an important message from his father. Mr. Rodney told Caesar to study hard and learn as much as he could. He gave him advice about friends. He

The Delaware River was alive with the comings and goings of huge ships filled with cargo, sailors, and stories from faraway places. Caesar enjoyed spending time at the harbor and was always anxious to sight a ship from home with its cargo of letters and packages sent by both family and friends.

told him to be careful to choose who he was close to. Wrong friends could bring trouble. Caesar took his father's advice and followed it for the rest of his life. He made many friends.

Later, Caesar's adult friends became important people in the colonies. Even today some of their names are famous.

Caesar lived in a boardinghouse–a private home that worked like a mini-hotel. Caesar's parents paid the owner of the boardinghouse. In exchange, Caesar received room and board. In other words, he had a place to sleep and eat. This was where Caesar lived while he attended Latin School.

Latin School in Philadelphia was like other Latin schools in the colonies. Students learned foreign languages such as Latin and Greek. They also learned elementary subjects like reading, writing, and math.

Caesar learned by reading many books. The books were not like today's colorful picture books. They were mostly black and white, with few or no pictures. It was difficult work. Caesar memorized grammar rules and pages of foreign languages. He recited sentences out loud in front of the class. He learned how to speak clearly in front of a group. This skill would be important later in his life.

Students had to perform their tasks perfectly. If they made even a tiny mistake, the punishment was harsh. Schoolmasters embarrassed the children. Classrooms often had a cone-shaped hat with an insult written on it. The child had to wear the hat and sit on a stool in the corner. But these punishments were the easy ones. Some schoolmasters beat the children with sticks, sometimes even making them go outside to select the stick first.

Even though Latin schools were demanding, wealthy families all over the colonies sent their boys there. Children in Europe had been learning this way for over 100 years. The books exposed children to the great thinkers. This kind of learning was called a classical education. Parents believed that the difficult work would build strong character in their sons. They hoped that this kind of education would prepare their children to lead successful lives.

Caesar studied hard. He spent up to eight hours a day in class. He went to writing school too. A page of his practice writing still survives over 250 years later.

Things went smoothly for Caesar. But when he got sick it was hard to be so far from home. In the summer of 1743 he received a letter from his father. Mr. Rodney wrote that he was sorry Caesar didn't feel well. But he had good news for his son. His mother was planning to visit him in the fall. That news cheered Caesar up. So did the news that came a few months later. Caesar's mother was going to have another baby.

Caesar didn't have much free time. When he did get a free moment, he and his friends loved to see the sights in Philadelphia. Sometimes Caesar met his friends in the State House yard, a large green park about five blocks from the river. They enjoyed the fresh air of the park and watching the people. They hoped to catch sight of some Indians. Indian chiefs sometimes stayed in the State House when they were in town for meetings. The

The State House was considered one of the most impressive buildings in the colonies.

State House yard was a great place for the people of Philadelphia to see and be seen.

The new Pennsylvania State House was the the most impressive government building in the colonies. The red brick, two-story building was graceful and elegant. Five marble steps led to a large door. Over the door was the British royal **coat of arms.** It stood for the power of the

English king over the 13 colonies. A large bell in the tower rang out to call the people. People gathered in the yard to hear important news announced.

Fourteen-year-old Caesar stood in the yard and admired the State House. He didn't know that 33 years later he would rush up those steps to an important meeting. He had no idea that his future would be forever linked with this building.

In 1745, when Caesar was 17, his world was rocked by the death of his father. Caesar attended the funeral at his home in Delaware. Afterward, he looked with sadness at his three little brothers. Baby Thomas, not even one year old, would grow up never knowing his father.

Now Caesar had to take full responsibility for the plantation and the family. Because of this, no one knows how much education he completed. He was not known as a scholar in later years, so he probably didn't finish his schooling. But he put his education to good use.

Caesar had reached a turning point in his life. His father had chosen a man by the name of Nicholas Ridgely to be Caesar's guardian. Under this man's guidance, Caesar began to learn about the laws of Delaware. Caesar liked what he learned, and spent the next 10 years running the plantation while learning about the government of the three lower counties of Delaware.

In 1754 the French and Indian War broke out in the colonies. The British and the French had been fighting in Europe for a long time. Their colonies were next to each other in America. The French and Indians joined forces to fight the British. The colonists got involved because they were subjects of the king of England. Caesar continued to work the family plantation while he waited for news of the war.

In the spring of 1755, Caesar began to get involved in running his county. With the French and Indian War going on, the people of Delaware needed to protect themselves. Caesar wrote a letter inviting the citizens of his county to form a **militia** and to choose officers. These men were called upon when they were needed in Delaware.

When he was 27, Caesar landed a job as high sheriff of Kent County. He also developed asthma. Though this sometimes made breathing difficult, Caesar carried out his duties faithfully. One of his responsibilities was making sure that landowners got paid by the people who owed them money. Once Caesar had to seize land from a man who didn't pay his bills. This bold move showed that Caesar was not afraid to act out his duties.

When the Delaware militia formed, Caesar became a captain serving under Colonel John Vining. Despite increased difficulty breathing, Caesar trained the militia every day. One day he met the colonel's daughter, Mary. Caesar called her Molly. He fell in love with her and wrote her a love letter. But something went wrong. Maybe she never got the letter, perhaps her parents had other plans for her, or maybe she didn't love

Caesar. No one knows why, but Molly married somebody else. She died less than a year later. Caesar was heartbroken.

Caesar threw himself into his work. He earned the respect of the people of Delaware. They chose him to be a **delegate** to their House of Assembly.

The colonists made their laws in the assembly, where meetings took place to talk about important matters. Because every colonist couldn't attend, they elected a few trustworthy delegates to go in their place. The delegates served for one year and had to be reelected every year they served.

Caesar worked hard for the people who elected him. During the next 15 years, he held over 10 government jobs, many of them at the same time. His dedication to his work would be proved again and again as the colonies began a difficult time of struggle with the king of England.

Angered by a tax on tea, a group of
colonists boarded a ship in Boston Harbor
one evening. Disguised as Native Americans, the colonists threw the ship's valu-
able cargo of tea into the sea. This event
later became known as the Boston Tea
Party.

3
Trying to Keep the Peace

The year 1760 was very eventful. England's war with the French continued in Europe, but most of the fighting in the American colonies had ended. Caesar was delighted the fighting was over. Now he could turn his attention back to his beloved plantation and his many government jobs.

This was also the year when a new king–George III–took the throne of England. When George was 10 years old, he was just beginning to learn to read. When he became king of England, he was just 22 years old, a young age to be running a country. He made some bad decisions, and he was stubborn.

George III was very young when he took the throne of England. He was not one to admit to making mistakes and his heavy-handed treatment of the colonies soon led to revolt.

George III was sure that kings never made mistakes.

Trouble began almost immediately when England tried to tighten control over the colonies. After all, England considered herself the "mother country," and her colonial "children" needed to be told what to do. The colonists disagreed.

Old English laws controlled many things, including taxes and trade. England even limited where the colonists could sell their goods. Many people had ignored these old laws for a long time. Now, England was about to force the colonists to obey them again.

A law called the Quartering Act annoyed some colonists. It forced them to provide housing and supplies to British soldiers. In England's opinion, the soldiers were sent to protect the colonists. Therefore, the colonists should pay for their stay.

Many colonists felt that the soldiers were only there to enforce the king's laws. What was worse, the colonists hadn't asked for the soldiers in the first place. So they didn't like the soldiers or the act. Children took to throwing stones and calling the red-uniformed soldiers names like "Redcoat" and "Lobsterback."

During this time, a very busy Caesar moved to Dover to be closer to his work. His youngest brother, Thomas, went with him. At this time, Caesar was running the plantation while serving as sheriff, justice of the peace, register of deeds, and also as a member of the assembly. In addition, the assembly asked him to work with another delegate to revise Delaware's laws.

Meanwhile, over in England, King George was worried that England's money was running low. The war with France had cost a lot, so he decided on a new tax. In 1765, he passed the Stamp Act. This meant that people had to buy a special colored stamp for every piece of paper they used.

The colonists were very unhappy about having to pay higher taxes. Everyone grumbled. The colonists had been making their own laws in their assemblies for a long time. They believed that the lawmakers in England didn't understand them. In fact, most English lawmakers had never even visited the colonies. And no colonists were allowed to help make English laws. Colonists hated this "taxation without representation." They stopped buying stamps. Some even attacked the men who sold the stamps, pouring hot, sticky tar over them and dumping feathers onto the tar. Because of this business with England suffered.

Now, for the first time, nine colonies joined together in a common cause. The Stamp Act had to go. The colonists planned a meeting that would take place in New York in October.

In 1765, England established the Stamp Tax. The tax was applied to every thing made of paper in the colonies— from newspapers to playing cards. Many colonists refused to pay these increased taxes.

They formed a **congress**, which became known as the Stamp Act Congress, and they picked their delegates with special care. The delegates needed to understand all sides of the problem. They needed to be smart, loyal, and bold as well as sensible. Delaware's assembly chose Caesar.

Caesar prepared to meet some of the most respected men in the colonies. His plantation would need constant attention, so he arranged for his younger brother Thomas to take over. Then he set off for New York.

Caesar and the other delegates met in New York on October 7, 1765. Caesar was impressed with all the delegates. He wrote to Thomas, saying that he was "in an Assembly of the greatest Ability" he "ever Yet saw." The delegates crafted letters to ask the king to **repeal** the Stamp Act. The meetings took far longer than expected. Caesar wrote often to Thomas. He explained that the situation was delicate and the delegates had to be careful with their words. They could not insult the king. Three weeks later the letters were shipped to England, and Caesar returned home to wait for the results.

Five months went by before they got their answer. England, pressured by its lagging commerce, ended the hated Stamp Act. The colonists were overjoyed. They celebrated with fireworks, parties, and bonfires. Caesar felt relieved about the new peace and hopeful about a better relationship with England.

The assembly elected Caesar and two other men to write another letter to the king. This was a fancy letter of thanks and loyalty. The king liked it so much that he read it twice.

The colonists celebrated a little too soon, however, for England passed another act. This one declared that England had the power to make laws for the colonies in all cases. Soon afterward, England began a new series of taxes on lead, glass, paper, paint, and tea. The colonists were furious. They decided to show their anger by not buying any of these products. In fact, they decided to **boycott** all English products.

This was a brave yet difficult move. Old laws had forbidden colonists to manufacture certain things. They depended on England to supply them. Now they had to learn to make these items themselves, or do without them. The colonists began to manufacture their own simple woolen cloth. They drank coffee instead of tea. Some made their own tea out of raspberry leaves. It wasn't as good, but colonists proudly drank their "liberty tea."

Caesar Rodney, and two other leaders from Delaware, Thomas McKean and George Read, wrote another letter, asking the king to repeal the new taxes. They also joined a committee of correspondence, which kept all the colonies informed about news.

Caesar was working so hard he had little time to pay attention to his health. His asthma was still a problem, and a sore on his face had been bothering him for some time. So, in June 1768, Caesar visited a doctor in Philadelphia. The doctor gave him devastating news: Caesar had cancer.

Caesar was scared. He wrote to Thomas, saying, "My case is truly dangerous." Thomas urged his brother to do whatever was necessary to be cured. Some friends told him to seek help in England, but a trip to England would take months. Caesar decided to instead get help in Philadelphia.

Dr. Thomas Bond performed the dangerous operation to remove Caesar's skin cancer. Ten days later, Caesar wrote to Thomas that the operation "has left a hole, I believe, quite to the bone, and extends for length from the corner of my eye above half way down my nose." Over time, doctors also applied powders to the cancer, but nothing completely cured it.

After the hole healed, it's believed that Caesar wore a green scarf over it when-

Sickness was a constant threat in colonial times. At times thousands died from smallpox, measles, or even influenza. Smallpox sometimes killed every child in a family. Diseases spread rapidly because strangers shared everything from drinking cups to beds. Viruses and germs hadn't been discovered yet. Fortunately, people learned to separate the sick and keep things clean. But they tried many treatments that seem odd today. A popular one was called "bleeding." The doctor made a small cut in the patient's arm and let a lot of blood drain out. This "bloodletting" even seemed to work. If it didn't, they tried again! Caesar received this treatment many times.

ever he was in public. He also began to wear a string of **amber** beads around his neck to ease his asthma. Years later, Caesar mentioned his cancer from time to time in letters to Thomas. He wrote that despite pain, fear, and embarrassment, Caesar never allowed himself to feel too sorry for himself. He was an **optimist.** His letters always showed strength of character and the hope that some day he would be well.

Caesar felt better after the operation, so he again turned to colonial affairs. He was soon elected speaker of Delaware's assembly. By the following year he was also serving as a judge in Delaware's supreme court. In the spring of 1770, Caesar was shocked to learn about the Boston Massacre.

Townspeople of Boston had been insulting and pushing around a redcoat. A crowd gathered and became violent. The redcoat called for help and was joined by nine English officers. During the noise and confusion, shots were fired. When the smoke cleared, five American colonists were

The Boston Massacre occured in 1770 when an argument between colonists and a British soldier quickly turned into a riot. During the confrontation, British soldiers opened fire on the crowd, leaving five dead.

dead. Caesar knew that peace with England was fading like the mists in the marshes.

That same year, England repealed all taxes except the tea tax. The king wanted to make a point, that England still had the right to tax them any way it pleased.

In 1771, Caesar's spirits sagged when he learned that he had lost his first election in 10 years. Maybe it was because of his illness. He certainly hadn't been able to spend as much time at his work as he liked. His brother Thomas thought there was another reason. He wrote to Caesar, reporting that he suspected an unfair vote. He made suggestions for improving voting practices in the next elections. The next year Caesar was again elected delegate for Delaware.

Meanwhile, up in Boston, angry colonists reacted to the tea tax. A group of men dressed up like Native Americans, crept onto British ships filled with tea, and dumped the tea into the dirty harbor. Proud colonists called it the Boston Tea Party.

England called it **treason.** The king punished Boston by closing and blocking the harbor. The people of Boston were in big trouble. Without supplies, they would soon starve.

Again, the 13 colonies banded together. A general congress would meet in Philadelphia in

September of 1774. Delaware decided on three delegates–Caesar Rodney, George Read, and Thomas McKean. Caesar first sent letters throughout Delaware to collect money and supplies for the people of Boston. At the end of August, he packed his bags for another trip to Philadelphia.

The First Continental Congress met in 1774 to try to ease tensions between the colonies and England. Their suggestions apparently went unheard as British forces moved into action soon thereafter, and in 1775, the first shots of the Revolutionary War were fired at the battles of Lexington and Concord.

4

Toward Independence

aesar arrived in Philadelphia a few days later, after "a very warm and disagreeable ride." He and the other delegates spent the weekend getting to know each other.

Caesar met Massachusetts delegate John Adams on Saturday. Mr. Adams later wrote, "Caesar Rodney is the oddest looking man in the world; he is tall, thin and slender as a reed, pale; his face is not bigger than a large apple, yet there is sense and fire, spirit, wit, and humor in his countenance."

The delegates met in the elegant City Tavern. They discussed where to hold the meetings. Two buildings had been offered, the State House and Carpenters Hall. The delegates wanted to honor Philadelphia's laborers, so they chose Carpenters Hall.

The Continental Congress began working on a warm Monday, on September 5, 1774. Caesar wrote to Thomas, who by now was also involved in Delaware politics. Caesar told him that more strangers were in town "than ever was known at any one time." The delegates agreed to keep their meetings secret. They kept the windows closed so people outside couldn't hear. Doorkeepers allowed only the delegates and messengers to enter.

Caesar had been feeling "very poorly" ever since he came to town, but he didn't miss meetings. Caesar was impressed with the delegates, especially the men from Virginia. He wrote to his brother, "All the seven delegates appointed for Virginia are here, and more sensible fine fellows you'd never wish to see, in short it is the greatest assembly that ever was Collected in America."

The delegates got right to work. In the middle of discussions about Boston Harbor, a tired messenger arrived. The news he brought from Boston was frightening. The British had taken 500 pounds of gunpowder from the Americans. Furthermore, their general was gathering and storing cannons. It looked as if England was preparing for war.

Congress advised all colonies to form militias and to begin preparing for war. Americans had been trading again with England because some acts had been repealed. This had to stop. Congress started another boycott. This one, though, would be enforced. Anyone found trading with England would be punished. Many congressmen still held out hope of peace, however. They formed committees to write more letters to the king.

Caesar reported the news to Thomas, claiming that even though he was sick, he never missed a day in Congress. He described his committee's tasks. Their letter would include the following: a list of the colonies' rights, what England had done to deny those rights, and polite suggestions on how England could patch up their friendship.

Philadelphians wanted to thank the delegates. They planned a huge party at the State House for the entire Congress. Caesar looked forward to it. He told Thomas, "It's intended to be the greatest [e]ntertainment that ever was made in this city."

Congress finished after a month of hard work. They made plans to meet again in the spring if relations with England didn't improve.

Caesar went home and was reelected by Delaware's Assembly. He worked for Delaware's independence from Pennsylvania. The two colonies had been linked together ever since William Penn had owned them. Caesar worked with the hope that things would get better. Instead, things got worse.

In April 1775, more than 600 English troops in Boston began a march to Concord, a nearby town. They planned to seize more gunpowder and arrest two **Patriots,** Sam Adams and John Hancock. Their pipers and drummers played a song along the way to insult the Americans. The song was "Yankee Doodle." A man named Paul Revere and two other Patriots rode to alert the colonists.

About 70 Americans met the "Lobsterbacks" in the early morning in Lexington, a town right next to Concord. No one knows who fired first, but shots echoed across the village green. Eighteen Americans lay bleeding on the ground, eight dead and ten wounded. It was April 19, 1775. The war had begun.

British troops marched on to Concord for the gunpowder. The colonists had hidden it well. The British couldn't find it. They started a few small fires. Their soldiers shot at the Americans who gathered. Americans shot back, and continued shooting as the British left town. In the battle of Concord, almost two English soldiers died for every American killed. After that, Americans began to sing "Yankee Doodle" with pride.

The following month, Caesar and the other delegates traveled to Philadelphia for the Second Continental Congress. Along the way, people waved their hats and cheered. Five hundred American soldiers met the delegates outside the city. They rode the rest of the way together. Philadelphia welcomed the delegates with a band and a grand parade. This time, Congress would gather in the State House.

Meetings began on the morning of May 10, 1775. Months of difficult work lay ahead. Some people believed the time had come to break the ties with England. These were the Patriots, or Whigs. Others felt that England was still the greatest country in the world. They wanted to stay loyal to England. These people were called **Loyalists,** or Tories. Still others wanted independence but felt that it was too soon to act. They wanted the colonies to wait until they were better prepared to break away.

Congress met every morning at nine o'clock. The delegates worked until three-thirty, some-

In the midst of war with England, the Second Contintental Congress would meet daily and debate whether the colonies should proclaim their independence from England.

times until five. Over time, some delegates became friends. Caesar's friends included George Washington and Richard Henry Lee. Every day, these three men met five other delegates for supper at the City Tavern. A table was reserved just for them. They often continued their discussions until after dark.

Days in Congress stretched to weeks. Because of the recent fighting, an urgent letter came from Massachusetts. It begged Congress to send someone to take charge of their militia. In June, Caesar wrote to Thomas, "We have appointed Coll. George Washington General and Commander in Chief of all the Colony forces." Mr. Washington agreed on one condition, that he receive no salary for his work. George Washington set off at once for Massachusetts.

Three months later, Caesar was promoted to brigadier general of the Kent County militia. With continued fighting in Boston at Bunker Hill, Caesar became more determined than ever for independence. He wrote to Thomas, "Continuing to Swear Allegiance to the power that is Cutting our Throats is certainly absurd."

Weeks in Congress stretched to months. By June 1776, several things had happened. All the colonies had begun to set up independent gov-

A close friend of Caesar's, George Washington was proclaimed commander in chief of the colonies' armed forces and led them in their fight for independence against the British.

ernments, calling themselves the United Colonies. Then Richard Henry Lee proposed that the colonies "ought to be free and independent States." This caused an uproar. Some congressmen still weren't ready to make the break. So Congress decided to wait three weeks before voting. They picked five men to work on a written declaration in case they might need it. Thomas Jefferson, known for his intelligence and skillful writing, was chosen to write the rough copy. Then Congress ended for a few weeks.

About that time, Caesar received alarming news. Back in Delaware, a large group of Tories had gathered. They were threatening to take over the government. Caesar knew he had to head home to Delaware.

On July 1, Congress met to vote on Lee's proposal. Independence would be a dangerous step, so it was important for all the colonies to agree. As Caesar explained, "Our union is our strength." Congress took a test vote. The results were: nine states in favor, two against, New York undecided, and Delaware split, with McKean in favor and Read against. Caesar, still in Delaware, was desperately needed to break the tie.

Congress decided to take the real vote the next day. McKean hurried out of the State House. He sent an urgent message to Caesar, explaining the situation. He begged Caesar to return to Philadelphia as soon as possible.

In the middle of the night, Caesar was awakened by a pounding on the door. He opened it. In trudged a tired rider with McKean's message. Caesar must get to Philadelphia before the vote! Caesar thought for a moment.

He was almost 48 years old. His cancer and his constant traveling were a strain. He was tired. The 80-mile trip to Philadelphia usually took about two days. He didn't have that much time. Riding at night would slow him down. Furthermore, the hot, muggy weather threatened rain. His asthma might flare up, and he might not make it in time. But his country needed him. Caesar called for his horse.

Did Caesar take a carriage on his famous ride? If so, why do images show him on horseback? Caesar's brother said he called for his carriage. A carriage provided shelter and an easier ride. But it was slower than horseback and risky in mud. Many people think Caesar rode a horse. Thomas McKean remembered that Caesar arrived tired, dusty, and covered with mud. It's possible that Caesar did both, starting with a carriage and later switching to a horse. It's probably not important *how* he got there. What *is* important is that Caesar *did*. Despite illness, Caesar gave up a night of sleep and rode through a thunderstorm for independence.

In terrible heat and almost total darkness, Caesar rode hard along dusty roads. His horse stumbled on stones and holes in the path. The weather turned nasty, and a storm broke overhead. There was no time to take shelter. Caesar galloped on. Wind howled. Rain slashed at the sore on his face. Dust turned to mud, which dragged at the horse's hooves and splattered all over Caesar. Thunder boomed and lightning crackled across the sky. The horse was terrified. They raced through towns and villages, slipping on rain-slicked cobblestones. Caesar only stopped when the

Caesar arrived in Philadelphia without a minute to spare to cast his vote for independence. This statue in Wilmington, Delaware, depicts that ride.

horse grew tired. He switched to a fresh horse and hurried on.

Hours later, the sky lightened and the storm passed. Caesar hadn't slept at all that night. He rode on, growing more tired with each passing hour. Sometime in the late afternoon, he spotted Philadelphia. Caesar sagged in relief. But was he too late? He raced up to the State House and dashed up the steps.

With Caesar's deciding vote cast, the Continental Congress asked Thomas Jefferson to draft a document to make their decision final. On July 4, 1776, the members adopted the document he created—the Declaration of Independence.

For Love of
Country

A man stopped Caesar at the door. Caesar showed him his papers, so the doorkeeper let him pass. Thomas McKean was waiting for him. They walked into the hot, stuffy room. At the sound of the door, all heads turned. Caesar stood in the doorway. His clothes were rumpled, dusty, and covered with mud. His usually pale face was flushed with heat. He stood still a moment to catch his breath, then strode into the room.

It was time for the vote. Caesar had gotten there just in time. At his turn, Caesar stood and voted for independence. He broke Delaware's tie. No one is sure what his exact words were. Years later, Thomas McKean wrote that Caesar said something like, "As I believe the voice of my constituents and of all sensible and honest men is in favor of independence and my own judgement concurs with them, I vote for independence." When the last vote was counted, 12 colonies had voted for independence. New York didn't vote because its delegates needed to wait for new instructions from their colony.

Attention now turned to Jefferson's written declaration. Some congressmen didn't like some of the wording. Congress worked on the changes the following day.

On the afternoon of July 4, 1776, the declaration was ready for a vote. All colonies, except New York, voted in favor of Jefferson's declaration. After the declaration was signed by John Hancock and Charles Thompson it was taken to a printer and copies were made. The copies were sent throughout the colonies.

On July 8, at exactly 12 o'clock, the bell in the State House tower began ringing the news of independence. People packed the State House yard. A man in uniform appeared. Silence fell. The man read the declaration to the gathering. When he finished the crowd cheered, "Huzza! Huzza! Huzza!" They celebrated with a parade. Bells clanged again. From then on, both the bell and the State House had new names. Today, people come from around the world to visit the Liberty Bell and Independence Hall in Philadelphia.

Philadelphians tore down the British coat of arms over the State House door. That night they tossed it into a bonfire. They watched the symbol of England's power go up in flames.

One week later, New York added its vote for independence. That made it unanimous, with all 13 colonies united. The declaration spread across the land. It was read over and over to the people of the new United States of America.

Caesar returned to Delaware and called a meeting of the Assembly. Its members finished

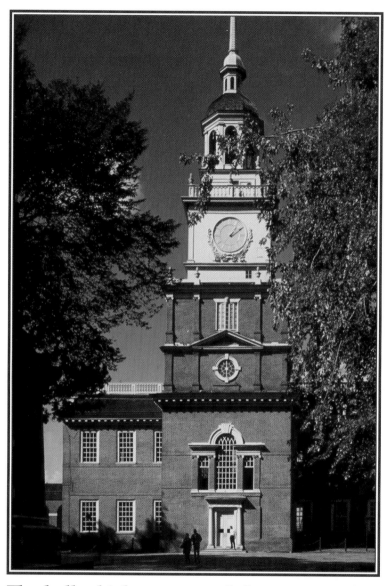

The bell which announced the signing of
the Declaration of Independence on July 8,
1776, was renamed the Liberty Bell, and
the State House became known as Independence Hall.

colonial business and set up Delaware as an independent state. Election time was near, but Caesar couldn't stay. Important business waited in Philadelphia, so Caesar left Delaware at the end of July.

On August 2, Caesar rejoined the Continental Congress. The declaration lay on a table in the center of the room. It was missing only one thing, the signatures that would make it complete. Every delegate knew he was about to take a very dangerous step. With signatures, the king could declare each man a traitor and have him hanged.

It was a serious moment. One by one, each man added his name to the paper that might become his doom. Caesar walked to the table and picked up the feather pen. He dipped it in the inkwell and signed his name. The document was ever after known as the Declaration of Independence. It became, and still is, one of the most important papers the world has ever known.

Delaware's election was held while Caesar was still away. By now, Tories held many offices. Their power caused Caesar to lose the election. Caesar's feelings were deeply hurt. He planned to "leave the public, and take the private paths of Life."

Family and friends wrote and begged him not to give up. Their support helped ease Caesar's pain. Still feeling a little betrayed, he wrote to Thomas Jefferson, "future Generations will Honor those names, that are neglected by the present Race."

Caesar now found more time to fight for his country. The news about recent battles was not good. The British had plenty of supplies and soldiers. Their well-trained troops far outnumbered the Americans. The Americans had lost several important battles. They were beginning to lose confidence. By the sounds of things, George Washington needed his help. Caesar turned to his military duties with new spirit.

The American army was in terrible shape. Soldiers were in short supply. A man who joined the Contintental army was paid very little. Sometimes his paycheck didn't come at all. In addition, he had to provide his own uniform and gun. The army couldn't provide them. Once joined, the soldier faced a miserable situation. He often made long, tiring marches with little or no food, shelter, or clothing. Sickness, disease, and death spread through the camps. Many soldiers died. Others ran away. Caesar worked hard to fill the need for troops. He talked people into joining the cause of freedom.

Caesar's responsibility was to keep the army outfitted and supplied with food. At times he had to spend his own money to accomplish this difficult task.

The American army needed more than soldiers. Everything was in short supply, including food, salt to keep meat from spoiling, cloth for uniforms, shoes, blankets, guns, gunpowder, and bullets. Caesar, now brigadier general, wrote many letters to get these things for the troops. At times he even used his own money when government money ran low.

Caesar was made commander of the post at Trenton, New Jersey. His main job was to organize and send troops to officers in battle. Caesar wasn't happy in this role—he wanted to do even more. He felt better after he received a special letter from George Washington. Washington praised Caesar's "readiness, industry, and alertness." He went on to say that these qualities "reflect the highest honour on your character."

In the summer of 1777, over 200 enemy ships appeared in Delaware Bay. Caesar thought they might attack Philadelphia. He placed guards to keep watch. He also ordered all the area's wagons, cattle, and flour to be hidden. This kept useful things out of the enemy's hands.

Within a few months the British invaded Delaware. They entered Wilmington and captured Delaware's governor who was called "president." Delaware needed another president, so the Assembly elected Thomas McKean. He promoted Caesar to Major General.

Shortly after that, Caesar was reelected as delegate to Congress. Caesar was delighted. But his highest honor was yet to come.

In March 1778, the people of Delaware elected Caesar Rodney as their new president. He served as president of Delaware for three-and-a-half years.

During this time, the situation for the American army was getting better. They had won some major battles. In October 1781, the largest British army waved the white flag of defeat and surrendered to George Washington at Yorktown. Even though the war was basically over, it would be a few more years until a **treaty** ended it forever.

Caesar was now feeling tired and sick. His years of travel, stress, and unending work had worn him out. The cancer was back and was worse than ever. Caesar returned to Philadelphia for medical help. The doctors did what they could.

Caesar still wrote cheerfully to his brother Thomas, who was married and had a son. The son's name was Caesar A. Rodney, in honor of his uncle. Caesar Rodney loved his nephew.

Caesar was in Delaware in the fall of 1783 when he was elected speaker of the Assembly again. Though now very sick, Caesar faithfully carried out his duties. By springtime he was too ill to go to meetings. In April the Assembly honored Caesar one last time. They brought the meeting to him.

Caesar Rodney died two months later, on June 26, 1784. He was 55 years old.

Caesar had been a good leader. He believed in honesty, fairness, and respect for all. He worked tirelessly for his people. He helped lead them from a collection of colonies to a united country. His brother Thomas may have said it best, when he claimed, "In truth he was a genuine Patriot and was guided solely by his love of justice, liberty and his country."

GLOSSARY

amber a golden-colored gem of fossilized tree sap

boycott a refusal to do business with another group

coat of arms a group of designs, usually in the shape of a shield, that represents a family

colony a group of people living in a new land but tied by law to their old country

congress a lawmaking group

delegate a person chosen to represent a larger group

Loyalists American colonists who wanted to remain part of England; also called Tories

militia citizen-soldiers used in emergencies

optimist a person who tends to think the best of things

Patriots American colonists who wanted independence from England; also called Whigs

plantation a large farm

repeal to take away

shallop a light, open boat

treason a threat to a government or ruler, often punishable by imprisonment or death

treaty a formal agreement between groups

CHRONOLOGY

1728 Caesar Rodney is born on October 7.

1743 Attends Latin School in Philadelphia.

1745 Caesar's father dies.

1756 Caesar begins a series of public service jobs, beginning with high sheriff of Kent County.

1758 Chosen as delegate to Delaware's Assembly.

1765 Works to end the Stamp Act at the Stamp Act Congress.

1768 Discovers he has cancer.

1769 Becomes Supreme Court justice and speaker of the Assembly.

1774 Attends the First Continental Congress.

1775 Serves in the Second Continental Congress.

1776 Rides to Philadelphia, votes for independence, signs the Declaration of Independence.

1777 Promoted to major general in the Revolutionary War.

1778 Elected president of Delaware.

1784 Dies at his home on June 26.

COLONIAL TIME LINE

1607 Jamestown, Virginia, is settled by the English.

1620 Pilgrims on the *Mayflower* land at Plymouth, Massachusetts.

1623 The Dutch settle New Netherlands, the colony that later becomes New York.

1630 Massachusetts Bay Colony is started.

1634 Maryland is settled as a Roman Catholic colony. Later Maryland becomes a safe place for people with different religious beliefs.

1636 Roger Williams is thrown out of the Massachusetts Bay Colony. He settles Rhode Island, the first colony to give people freedom of religion.

1682 William Penn forms the colony of Pennsylvania.

1688 Pennsylvania Quakers make the first formal protest against slavery.

1692 Trials for witchcraft are held in Salem, Massachusetts.

1712 Slaves revolt in New York. Twenty-one blacks are killed as punishment.

1720 Major smallpox outbreak occurs in Boston. Cotton Mather and some doctors try a new treatment. Many people think the new treatment shouldn't be used.

1754 French and Indian War begins. It ends nine years later.

1761 Benjamin Banneker builds a wooden clock that keeps precise time.

1765 Britain passes the Stamp Act. Violent protests break out in the colonies. The Stamp Act is ended the next year.

1775 The battles of Lexington and Concord begin the American Revolution.

1776 Declaration of Independence is signed.

FURTHER READING

Fradin, Dennis. *The Thirteen Colonies*. Chicago: Children's Press, 1988.

Fritz, Jean. *Will You Sign Here, John Hancock?* New York: Paperstar, Penguin Putnam Books for Young Readers, 1976.

Gauch, Patricia Lee. *This Time, Tempe Wick?* New York: G. P. Putnam, 1974.

King, David C. *Colonial Days*. New York: Wiley, 1998.

Knight, James E. *Seventh and Walnut, Life in Colonial Philadelphia*. New Jersey: Troll, 1982.

McGovern, Ann. *... If You Lived in Colonial Times*. New York: Scholastic, 1992.

Moore, Kay. *... If You Lived at the Time of the American Revolution*. New York: Scholastic, 1997.

INDEX

INDEX

PICTURE CREDITS

ABOUT THE AUTHOR

SUSAN MCCARTHY MELCHIORE lives in Pennsylvania with her husband and three children. She speaks three languages and holds a degree in Spanish education. She taught for six years in the Pennsylvania school system before leaving to raise her growing family and to begin writing seriously. This is her first book for children.

Senior Consulting Editor **ARTHUR M. SCHLESINGER, JR.** is the leading American historian of our time. He won the Pulitzer Prize for his book *The Age of Jackson* (1945) and again for *A Thousand Days* (1965). This chronicle of the Kennedy Administration also won a National Book Award. He has written many other books including a multi-volume series, *The Age of Roosevelt.* Professor Schlesinger is the Albert Schweitzer Professor of the Humanities at the City University of New York, and has been involved in several other Chelsea House projects, including the REVOLUTIONARY WAR LEADERS biographies on the most prominent figures of early American history.